BEST OF
Dave Matthews Band

Transcribed by Jimmy Kuehn
Cover photography by Danny Clinch
Interior photography by Sam Erickson

ISBN 1-57560-277-6

Visit our website at www.cherrylane.com

Carter Beauford

CONTENTS

ANTS MARCHING

Words and Music by
David J. Matthews

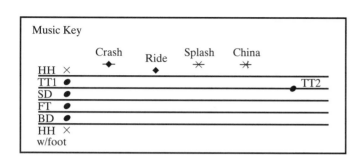

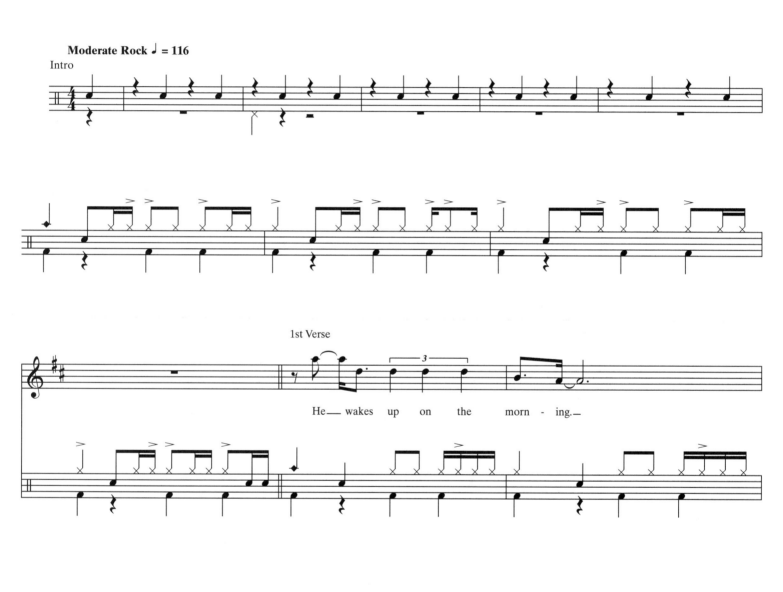

He— wakes up on the morn- ing.—

Does— his teeth, bite to eat and he's roll- ing. Nev- er chang- es— a

4

thing. The week ends, the week begins, she thinks.

We look at each other, won-d'ring what the oth-

er is think-ing. But we nev-er say a thing

and these crimes be-tween us grow deep-er.

5

Pre-chorus

ta - ble and dream - ing. Take these chanc - es,

place them in a box un - til a qui - et - er time. Lights

down, you up and die.

3rd Verse

Driv - ing a - long this high - way,— all— these cars and up -

on— the side - walk,— peo - ple in ev - 'ry di - rec - tion.—

No words ex - changed, no— time— to ex - change— a - when all—

Chorus

— the lit - tle ants— are march - ing, red— and black an - ten -

nae wav - ing. They all— do it the same,—

8

they all____ do it the same way,_____

_____ yeah.   Can - dy - man tempt - ing the thoughts of a

sweet tooth tor - tured, oh, by weight loss pro - gram, cut - ting the cor - ners,

loose end, loose end, cut,____ cut.   On the fence, could not____ to of - fend,

cut, cut, cut, cut. Take___ these___ chanc - es,_____

Pre-chorus

9

place them in a box un - til a qui - et - er time. Lights

down, you up and die.

Violin solo

Play 7 times

down, you up and die.

THE BEST OF WHAT'S AROUND

Words and Music by
David J. Matthews

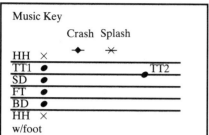

Moderate Funk ♩ = 97

1st Verse

Hey,— my friend,——

— it seems— your eyes— are trou-bled. Care to— share——

your time— with— me?——— Would you say— you're feel - ing—

— low? And— so— a good— i - dea— would be— to

Chorus

get it off your mind. ___ See, you and me ___ have a ___

___ bet-ter time ___ than most can dream. Have ___ it bet-ter than ___ the best, so ___

___ can a-pull on through ___ what-ev-er tears ___ at us,

what-ev-er holds ___ us down. And if ___ noth-ing can be done, ___ we'll make the

best of what's a-round. ___

Bridge

Turns out___ not where,___ but who you're with,___ that a - real - ly mat -

ters,___ that a - real - ly mat - ters.___

And hurts___ not much___ when you're___ a - round,___

___ when you're a - round.___ And if___ you hold___

2nd Verse

___ on___ tight to what___ you think___ is your thing,

you may__ find__ you're   miss - ing all__ the rest.__

Well, she run up__ in - to__ the__ light sur - prised.__ Her   arms__

__ are o - pen.__ Her__ mind's eye__ is...

Chorus

See - ing things__   from a__ bet - ter side__ than most can__ dream. On__

__ a clear - er road__ I feel,   oh,   you could say she's

15

safe. What-ev-er tears_ at her, what-ev-er holds_ her down._ And if_

_ noth-ing can be done,_ she'll make the best of what's a-round._

Bridge

Turns out_ not where_ but what you think,_ a-that a-real-ly mat-

ters,_ that a-real-ly mat-ters,_ that a-real-ly mat-

ters,_____ that a - real - ly mat - ters,_____ yeah._____

Sax solo

La,—

— la, la,— la, la,— la, la,— la, la,— la, la,— la, la,— la, la.

Chorus

See, you and me— have a— bet - ter time— than— most can dream. Have—

— it bet - ter than— the best, so— can a - pull on through—

— what - ev - er tears— at us, what - ev - er holds— us down.— And if—

— noth - ing can be done,— we'll make the best of what's a - round.—

—

*Lead vocal is doubled by background vocals till end.

*Voc. Fig. 1

*Includes lead and bkgd. vocals.

(end Voc. Fig. 1)

w/Voc. Fig. 1 (till end)

Begin fade

Fade out

CRASH INTO ME

you,   and I come in - to

you.

In a boy's   dream,

in a boy's   dream.

2nd Verse

Touch your lips just

so I know. In your eyes, love, it glows so. I'm

bare - boned and cra - zy for you.

Chorus

Oh, when you come crash in - to me,

yeah, ba - by. And I come in - to you.

you. In a boy's

dream,   in a boy's ——— dream.

Hmm,—

—— if I've ——— gone o - ver - board,—— and I'm

beg - ging you ——— to ——— for - give me,—— oh,—— in my haste.   I'm

hold - ing —— you so, girl,—————— close   to me.—— And you come

and show your world to me. In a boy's dream,

in a boy's dream.

Oh, I watch you there, through the win-dow, and I stare at you

wear noth-ing, but you wear it so well. Tied up and twist-ed, the

way I'd like to be. For you, for me, come crash in-to me, ba-

in - to me.— Please, crash a lit - tle babe.—

No, no,— no, oh, yes,—

— I see the wave— come and crash in - to me. See the wave— come and—

w/vocal ad lib (till end)

— crash in - to me.— Crash— in - to me.

Begin fade

Fade out

DON'T DRINK THE WATER

Words and Music by
David J. Matthews

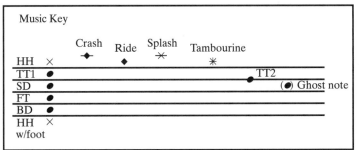

2nd Verse

A - way, a - way, you—

— have been— ban - ished.— Your—

— land— is gone— and— giv - en— me.

Pre-chorus

And here— I— will— spread my— wings.—

Yes, I— will call this

33

home.

Chorus

What's this— you say?— You feel— a right to— re - main?— Then stay and

w/vocal ad lib. (next 3 bars)

I will bur - y you.—

What's that— you say?—— Your

fa - ther's spir - it— still lives in— this place? Well, I will si - lence you.—

Here's— the hitch... Your— horse is— leav - ing.—

— Don't miss— your boat,— it's

leav - ing— now.

Pre-chorus

And as you go— I— will spread my— wings.—

Yes, I ___ will call this home. ___

Chorus

But I have ___ no time ___ to

jus - ti - fy ___ to you. ___ Fool, you're blind. Fool, move a - side for me. ___

All I ___ can say ___ to you, my new neigh - bor, is

you must_ move on   or   I   will   bur - y   you._____

w/vocal ad lib (next 2 bars)

Now   as   I

Bridge

rest   my___   feet   by_   this   fi - re...   Those_   hands_   once   warmed   here,_   but   I   have   re - tired_

___   them.   I   can   breathe_   my   own   air   and   I   can   sleep_   more___   sound - ly.___   Up -

on   these_   poor_   souls   I'll   build   heav - en   and   call   it

home,   'cause you're all dead

— now.   And I live with my jus - tice,   and I live with my

greed - y—— need. Oh, I live with no mer - cy,   and I live with my

fren - zied—— feed - ing. I live with my ha - tred,   and I live with my

jeal - ous - y. Oh, I live with the no - tion that may I don't need

Outro

an - y - one but— me.
(...an - y - one — but me.)

Don't— drink the wa - ter.—

Don't— drink the wa - ter.—

There's blood— in the wa - ter.—

Don't— drink the wa - ter. Me,————— yeah.

(And I live with my—

— jus - tice,——— and I live with my greed - y need.— And I live with no—

Don't— drink the wa - ter.— Don't— drink the wa - ter.—

— mer - cy,——— and I live with my fren - zied feed - ing. I live with my—

RAPUNZEL

Words and Music by
David J. Matthews, Stefan Lessard
and Carter Beauford

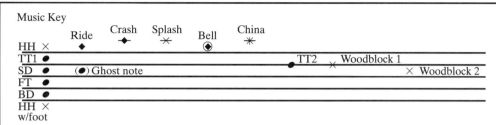

cious ____ per - fect lit - tle mouth,__ there_ up - on___ I lin -

ger. You_ will have_ no doubt__ that I'll_ do my best___ for_ you, I do.__

Love,__ let's_ stop to get it go - in'. Lost_ my - self_ just think - in' a - bout_ the two_ of us__

__ from_ each oth - er drink - in'. Be - gin with_ the lips,__ fin - ger - tips_ and kiss -

ing. Turn_ me in - side out,__ and I__ do my best__ for_ you.

44

you blow my head o - pen. Of one thing I'm sure,

that I'll do my best for you, I do.

Oh, for you I would crawl, through the dark - est dun -

geon. Climb the cas - tle wall if you're my Ra - pun -

zel. You let your hair down, right in through the win -

dow. Good they locked the door, 'cause I do my best

for you. Yuh.

Yuh. Oh.

Hmm. I think the

world of you, all my

Ah.

3rd Verse

Too—— good to be real,—— the smell—— of some-thing cook -

in'. My—— soul you're—— to steal,—— food—— of love—— we're fill -

ing.—— What—— you've giv-en me,—— for—— it there's—— no meas -

ure. Of—— one thing—— I know—— is I'll—— give my best—

49

car - ry your bur - dens too. And I give my

world to you.

Uh! Oh.

4th Verse

Hop, hip, lock up so tight you drive me cra - zy. Cra - zy is all right

51

w/sound effects and talking
(Approx. 15 sec.)

SATELLITE

Words and Music by
David J. Matthews

Chorus

Tom— for the— moth - er - sta - tion.— Win - ter's

mf

cold,_____ spring e - ras - es. And the

calm,_____ a - way— by the storm is— chas - en.

Ev - 'ry - thing good needs re - plac - ing.— Look up,

look down— all a - round. Hey,— sat - tel - lite.

2nd Verse

Sat - el - lite head - lines read.

— Some - one's se - crets you've seen, eyes— and ears— have

been. Sat - el - lite dish— in— my yard,—

tell me more, tell— me— more. Who's the— king— of your—

Chorus

sat - el - lite cas - tle?— Win - ter's cold,—

55

spring e-ras - es. And the calm,

— a - way— by the storm is— chas - en. Ev - 'ry - thing

good needs re - plac - ing.— Look up, look down—

all a - round. Hey,— sat - el - lite.

Bridge

Rest— high a - bove the cloud, no re -

stric - tion.___ Tel - e - vi - sion we bounce 'round the___

world.   And while___ I spend these hours,___ five sens -

es reel - ing,   I___ laugh a - bout this weath - er - man's___

sat - el - lite___ eyes.___

3rd Verse

Sat - el - lite   in my eyes,___ like a

diamond in the sky. How I won - der.

Sat - el - lite stray__ from__ the moon,__ and the

world your bal - loon. Peep - ing__ Tom__ for the__ moth - er__ sta -

Chorus

tion.__ Win - ter's cold,_____ spring e - ras -

es. And the calm,_____ a - way__ by

the storm is—chas - en. Ev- 'ry - thing good needs re -

plac - ing.— Look up, look down,— all a - round. Hey,—

— sat - tel - lite.

Bridge

Rest— high a - bove the cloud, no re - stric - tion.—

59

Tel - e - e - vi - sion we bounce 'round this— world.

And while— I spend these hours,— five sens - es reel - ing,

I— laugh a - bout this weath - er - man's— sat - el - lite—

eyes.—

SO MUCH TO SAY

Words and Music by
David J. Matthews, Boyd Tinsley
and Peter Griesar

61

can't___ see the light. O - pen___ up___ my head___

and_____ let___ me out,_____ a - lit - tle ba - by.___ 'Cause

Chorus

here we have been stand - in' for a long, long_____ time.___

Tread - in' trod - den trails for a long, long_____ time.___

2nd Verse

___ I say my hell is___ the

clos - et___ I'm___ stuck in - side.___ Can't___

___ see the light. And my heav - en is a

nice house_ in the sky.___ Got cen - tral heat - ing and I'm al - right.___ 'Cause

Chorus

here we have been stand - in' for a long, long___ time.___

Tread - in' trod - den trails for a long, long___ time,___

64

by. Lit - tle feet, a - lit - tle feet, a - lit - tle ba — by.___
(Lit - tle hands, lit - tle feet, lit - tle ba — by.)___

___ One year of cry - in' and the words___ creep up in - side,___ creep in - to your mind,___

Chorus

___ yeah.___ So much to say, so much___ to say, so much to

say, so much___ to say.___

So much to say, so much___ to say, so much to

say,   so much   to   say.   'Cause

Chorus

here   we   have   been   stand - in'   for   a   long,   long   time.

Tread - in'   trod - den   trails   for   a

long,   long   time,   time,   time,   time,   time,   time,

Bridge

time.   I   find   some - times   it's

eas - y___ to be my - self.___ Some - times___

I find it's bet - ter to be some - bod - y else.___

Chorus

So much to say, so much___ to say, so much to

say, so much___ to say.___ So much to say, so much___

___ to say, so much to say, so much___ to say.___

So much to say, so much to say, so much to

say, so much to say.

So much to say, so much to say, so much to

say, so much to say. O - pen up my head

and let me out, lit - tle ba - by.

STAY (WASTING TIME)

Words and Music by
David J. Matthews, Stefan Lessard
and Leroi Moore

as— sweat— ran down—— your face. Reached— up— and I

caught it at your— chin, licked— my fin - ger - tips. We were,

Chorus

we were...— Just wast - in'—— time. Let the ho-
(Ooh. Wast - in' time.

urs roll by,— do-in' noth - in' for— the fun.— A lit - tle— taste of the good—
Ooh.——————— Good—

— life, wheth-er right— or wrong,— makes us wan-na stay, stay,— stay,
— life. Right or wrong.— Stay,

70

stay, stay for a while.
stay, stay for a while.)

2nd Verse

Well, then la - ter on

the sun be - gan to fade. And then, well, the

clouds rolled o - ver our heads and it be - gan to rain.

Oh, we were danc - in', mouths o - pen, and you were splash -

in' in the tongue taste, and for a mo - ment this good

time would nev-er end. You and me, you and me. Just

Chorus

wast - in' time. I was kiss - in' you,
(Ooh. Wast - in' time. Kiss - in' you.

kiss - in' me, love, from a good day in - to the moon - light. Now a night
Ooh. Moon - light.

so fine, makes us wan-na stay, stay, stay, stay, stay for a while.
night so fine. Stay, stay, stay for a while.)

Interlude I

Makes— you wan-na, makes you wan-na...)

(Makes— me wan-na, makes you wan-na...)

(Don't— it make— you wan-na?)

Chorus

We are— wast - in'——

—— time.—— I— shall miss this— thing— when it all rolls by.— What a
(Ooh. All rolls by.)

—— day,—— and wan-na stay, stay,— stay,—— stay— for— a while.—

Interlude II

Chorus

Hey,———————— hey,——— love.——— Oh,———
(Hey, love.— Oh,—

— just grop-in' you,— roll-in' in the mud.— Stay———— a—
— just grop-in' you. Ooh,— oh,— oh yeah.— Stay— a while,

— while.— Oh, come on,——— I wan-na stay, stay,— stay,
see— the world. Come on,— girl.)

74

Sax solo/Outro

stay,   stay for a   while.

(Makes me wan-na, makes you wan-na

Bkgd. Voc. Fig. 1   (end Bkgd. Voc. Fig. 1)   w/Bkgd. Voc. Fig. 1 (7 times)

stay.   Makes me wan-na, makes you wan-na

Bkgd. Voc. Fig. 2

(end Bkgd. Voc. Fig. 2)

stay.   Don't   it___   make_ you   wan - na

w/Bkgd. Voc. Fig. 2 (13 times)

stay!)

TOO MUCH

Words by David J. Matthews
Music by David J. Matthews, Carter Beauford,
Stefan Lessard, Leroi Moore and Boyd Tinsley

I'm gon - na pack more lines so I can get down in.

2nd Verse

Oh, traf - fic jam got more cars than a beach got sand.

Suck it up, suck it up, zip, suck it up, fill it up, till no more.

I'm no cra - zy creep. I've got it com - ing to

me 'cause I'm not sat - is - fied. Hun - ger keeps on grow-ing.

Chorus

I eat— too much.—

— I drink— too much.— I want— too much.—

— Too much!

I've got this growl___ in my tum-my. I gon - na stop it to - day.___

Chorus

___ I eat___ too much.___ I drink___ too much.___

___ I want___ too much.___ Too___ much!___

ba - by.

'Cause I eat_ too much._

'Cause I drink_ too much._

'Cause I want_ too much._____

Too much!

Begin fade

I got - ta get it some - where._

Fade out

____

I eat_ too much._

WHAT WOULD YOU SAY

Words and Music by
David J. Matthews

you came tum-bling af-ter
('cause of o-rig – i-nal sin.)

Pre-chorus

Rip a-way the tears, drink a hope to hap-py years and

you may find a life-time's passed you by.

Chorus

What would you say? Don't drop the big one.
If you a mon-key on a

well, don't cut my life-line.
well, don't bite the mail-
string, If you a dog-gie on a chain,

88

man.—
What— would you say?—

2nd Verse

I was— there when— the bear— ate——— his head;— he— thought it was— can -

dy.
(Ev - 'ry - one goes— in the end.)
Knock,— knock on the door.— Who's—

— it for?— There's no - bod - y in—— here.
(Look in the mir - ror, my friend.)
I

Pre-chorus

don't un - der - stand,— at best, can - not speak— for all the rest. The

morn - ing rise,___ a life - time's passed__ me by.___

Chorus

What__ would you say?___ Don't drop the big___ one.
If you a mon - key on a

well, don't cut my life - line.___ well, don't bite the mail -
string, If you a dog - gie on a chain,

man.___ What__ would you say?___

Bridge

Ev - 'ry__ dog has its day, ev - 'ry__ day has its way of be - ing for - got - ten. *Mom, it's my
*Lead vocal is doubled
by bkgd. vocals, next 5 bars.

birth - day. Would you say,— hey?   What— would you   say?—

(Now, what would you   say?)—

Sax solo

Harmonica solo

3rd Verse

I was there when the bear ate his head, he thought it was candy. Ev-'ry-one goes

in the end. (end.) Knock, knock, on the door. Who's it for? There's no-bod-y in

here. (Look in the mir-ror, my friend.)

Pre-chorus

I don't un-der-stand, at

best, can-not speak for all the rest. The morn-ing rise, a life-

time's passed me by. What would you say?

HI-HAT

OPEN AND CLOSED HI-HAT: Strike the open hi-hat on notes labeled with an *o*. Strike the closed hi-hat on unlabeled notes.

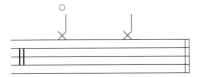

HI-HAT WITH FOOT: Clap hi-hat cymbals together with foot pedal.

HI-HAT WITH SLUR: The open hi-hat is struck and then closed with the foot on the beat indicated by the hi-hat w/foot notation below, creating a *shoop* sound.

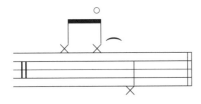

HI-HAT BARK: The open hi-hat is struck and is immediately, almost simultaneously closed so that the *shoop* sound is severely clipped.

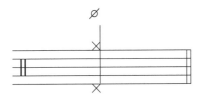

CYMBALS

CHOKE: Hit the crash cymbal and catch it immediately with the other hand, producing a short, choked crash sound.

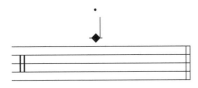

BELL OF CYMBAL: Hit the cymbal near the center, directly on the cup or bell portion.

CYMBAL ROLL: Play a roll on the cymbal rapidly enough to produce a sustained, uninterrupted *shhh* sound lasting for the number of beats indicated.

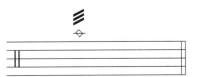

DRUMS

CROSS STICK: Anchor the tip end of the stick on the snare drum skin at the eight o'clock position, two to three inches from the rim. Then raise and lower the butt end, striking the rim at the two o'clock position, producing a clicky, woodblock-type sound.

FLAM: Hit the drum with both sticks, one slightly after the other, producing a single, thick-sounding note.

RUFF: Play the grace notes rapidly and as close to the principal note as possible. The grace notes are unaccented and should be played slightly before the beat. The principal note is accented and played directly on the beat.

CLOSED ROLL: Play a roll on the snare drum creating a sustained, uninterrupted *tshhh* sound lasting for the duration of the rhythm indicated and with no break between the two tied notes.